HUES OF METANOIA

AF651761

Published By

www.poetryworld.org

Hues of Metanoia
Written by Mansi Keswani
Published by: Poetry World Org.
Publisher's Address: Haryana
Printed under PWO in India

 Special credits to Dr.Niveditha and Dr.Nitin Chopra.

Edition: I (2025)
ISBN (Paperback) - 9789392507854
Book Design by POETRY WORLD

HUES OF METANOIA

MANSI KESWANI

m e t a n o i a

(meh-ta-noy-ah) ● Greek

(n.) the journey of changing one's mind, heart, self,

or way of life; spiritual conversion

HUES OF METANOIA

Step into a world where the mind's landscapes shift like seasons and the heart undergoes a slow, beautiful metamorphosis. This book is more than a mere collection—it's an intimate voyage through the evolving thoughts and emotions. Every poem, story, and piece of prose is a window into the author's soul, reflecting a depth of feeling that only time can carve.

Woven through these pages are the tender threads of love, the sharp edges of self-discovery, and the subtle tensions of societal norms. And let's not forget the political undercurrents that ripple beneath the surface, challenging you to think as much as you feel.

But don't expect a sombre read—humour winks at you from the corners, reminding us that even in the heaviest moments, there's room for a smile. This is a book that invites you to laugh, question, and journey inward as much as outward.

Whether you're seeking solace in poetry, wisdom in prose, or a tale that stays with you long after the last page is turned, this collection offers it all. It's a decade of life distilled into words—rich, reflective, and refreshingly real.

ACKNOWLEDGEMENTS

…………

As this journey of words finds its culmination in the form of a book, I find myself overwhelmed with gratitude.

First and foremost, I would like to express my heartfelt thanks to my parents, whose unwavering love and support have been the bedrock of my life. Your faith in me has been my constant source of inspiration.

To my teachers, who ignited the spark of curiosity within me, thank you for shaping my mind and encouraging my passion for writing. Your guidance has been invaluable.

I am deeply indebted to the Poetry World Organization for their belief in my work and for providing the platform to share my thoughts with a wider audience. Your support has been instrumental in bringing this book to fruition.

To my friends, who have walked alongside me through thick and thin, your companionship and encouragement have been a constant source of strength. Thank you for being my sounding board, cheerleaders, and confidantes.

A special mention goes to my cousin Yash, my accomplice in countless youthful escapades. One lazy afternoon, as boredom threatened to consume us, Yash suggested we experiment starting a blog. With a mix of scepticism and curiosity, I agreed. Little did I know, this casual suggestion would become the catalyst that would ignite my passion for writing. Yash, with his infectious enthusiasm, pushed me out of my comfort zone and into the uncharted territory of self-expression. His belief in my ability to articulate my thoughts gave me the courage to share my inner world.

Last but certainly not the least, I offer my sincerest gratitude to my guru, whose blessings have guided me on this path. Your wisdom and spiritual guidance have enriched my life in countless ways.

To everyone who has contributed to this book, directly or indirectly, thank you. Your presence in my life has made this journey extraordinary.

PREFACE

This book is an invitation to step into the labyrinth of my mind, a space where thoughts intertwine and evolve over a decade. It is here, in the raw and unfiltered pages that follow, I've laid bare the tapestry of my experiences, dreams, fears, and aspirations.

Writing has been my steadfast companion on this journey. It has served as a vessel for my emotions, a canvas for my imagination, and a mirror reflecting the complexities of my inner world. Through the rhythmic cadence of words, I have sought to understand myself, to connect with the world, and to find meaning in the chaos of existence.

These pieces are not polished gems, rather fragments of a life in progress. They are snapshots of a soul in flux, caught between the idealism of youth and the complexities of adulthood.

The reader will find here the echoes of youthful exuberance, the quiet contemplations of maturity, and the uncertainties that bridge the two. Much like a bildungsroman, it aims to trace the evolution of my mind as an author, exploring the intricate development of my writing style and perspective over time.

I have chosen to preserve the original form of these writings to offer an authentic portrayal of my growth. This book is not merely a collection of words, but a chronicle of transformation.

As you embark on this journey with me, I invite you to bring your experiences to the table. Let us explore together the intricate patterns woven within these pages, and may these words resonate deep within your soul.

This collection is a study in hues of metanoia—a kaleidoscope of transformations, each shade revealing a new facet of my evolving self. It is my hope that by sharing these intimate reflections, I can inspire others to embrace their journeys of growth and discovery.

These pages are an open invitation to witness the alchemy of thought and emotion as they coalesce into something tangible.

In sharing these vulnerabilities, I hope to create a space where readers can find solace, recognition, or simply a companionable silence.

Ultimately, this book is an exploration of the human condition, a quest for meaning in a world often shrouded in uncertainty. It is a reminder that growth is a lifelong journey, marked by both triumphs and setbacks. And it is a testament to the enduring power of the written word to connect, heal, and inspire us.

FOREWORD

....

At dawn, the birds herald a new day, the old proverbial rooster has snuck back into slumber on the night far removed. So come the trilling chorus of muse-ridden bards enchanting the dawn, awakening the sweeping spectra of hues- that evolve the soul to its glorious renditions of spiritual quest. Wade, walk or wallow into the myriad visions of a darling yet daring poetess, philosopher and princess of literature- she will enthral you to your origins. Meet Mansi in her solitary stations on a solo journey through her span of time. Her words not yours or mine will latex gold straight out of mundane rock of civilisation, enmeshed, ensnared and enamoured to perdition, with HOPE forever.

- School life mentor: Ashok Doss

1| Dear home

Dear Home,

The bricks that hold you together are far more than mere mortar and stone; they are fragments of time, pieces of memory lovingly etched into every corner.

I know, I know—I was so eager to leave, wasn't I? Always dreaming of the new, the unknown, of life beyond your walls. I couldn't wait to move to a bigger, better space, impatient to say goodbye to all the little inconveniences you held. And yet, here I am now, sitting in my new house, overcome by a wave of nostalgia so strong it feels like a bittersweet hug from the past.

How foolish I was to think I wouldn't miss you. Perhaps my constant complaints about your imperfections were just a way to shield myself, to avoid confronting how much leaving you would hurt. After all, you weren't just a house—you were a witness to my entire life.

You saw it all, didn't you? The quiet beginnings of dreams, the moments of courage, and the small joys that grew into cherished memories.

You were there when my love for literature first bloomed, when books and stories filled your quiet corners with magic. You stood by me as my fears grew too, even the smallest ones, like my irrational dread of insects, which somehow always found their way to your nooks. You even turned me into a gardener, as I poured my heart into beautifying your space, not realizing I was creating a bond that would be so hard to break.

And now, I've learned you've stood tall for over four decades, carrying not just our family but the weight of generations before us. It feels so strange to think of you without us now. You must be so quiet, so still—without our laughter, our tears, our arguments, or our celebrations to fill your spaces. The thought makes my heart ache.

Oh, dear home, Every creak in your floor, every crack in your walls, and every patch of sunlight that fell through your windows carried stories—stories that are now woven into the very fabric of who I am.

But life moves forward, doesn't it? This new house is a new beginning—a blank canvas waiting to be painted with fresh memories and new dreams. Yet no matter how bright this new chapter may be, the pages written in your embrace will always hold a special place in my heart.

Dear home, you will forever be my sanctuary, my anchor to a time when life felt simpler and fuller all at once. The memories we created within your walls will be cherished for a lifetime, carried forward like a warm light into the new.

With all my love,
Mansi

2| The Mind's Pendulum

A pendulum of thought, the mind does sway,
Between the heavens and the earthly clay.
With force it climbs, a soaring, hopeful flight,
Then gravity reclaims its rightful might.

To cease its rhythm is a barren state,
A stagnant pool where thoughts stagnate and wait.
It craves the tempest, the ecstatic rise,
And the descent that humbles and chastise.

A tender keeper is the soul required,
To shield it from the world's corrosive mire.
Too tight a grip, it suffocates and dies,
Too loose a hold, it's lost to careless skies.

A delicate balance, a precarious art,
To nurture growth, yet play a careful part.
For, in this swing, the universe resides,
A cosmic dance where consciousness abides.

3| Inner Compass

Is truth a phantom, dancing in the night,
A hidden treasure, out of mortal sight?
Or does it reside, a flame within the heart,
A guiding compass, setting souls apart?

A fragile vessel, easily overthrown,
Or a steadfast anchor, firmly rooted and grown?
A secret held by those in lofty towers,
Or a common gift, in life's most precious hours?

A fleeting mirage, an illusion's art,
Or a solid ground, where souls can find their part?

A pawn in games of power, wealth, and might,
Or a guiding star in life's uncertain night?
A luxury for few, a privilege rare,
Or a universal right, beyond compare?

Like musk deer seeking scent in distant lands,
We often search for truth in foreign hands.
But truth, its whispers, resides deep within,
A quiet knowing, free from worldly din.

Seek not the answer in the outer sphere,
For truth's profoundest depths are centered here.
Within the soul's mysterious, sacred space,
Resides the wisdom, time cannot erase.

4| The Intangible Barriers

They speak of walls, of borders drawn,
Of war's harsh lines and battles won.
Of caste that cut, and culture clash,
Divisions marked by history's lash.

But deeper still, a darkness lies,
In hearts where truth is veiled by lies.
The prideful ego, ever strong,
That blinds us to where we belong.

The mind that shuns its own reflection,
A twisted path, a life's deflection.
The empty claim, the love unshown,
Are the barriers of our own.

Let fall the walls of self-made night,
Embrace the truth, and see the light.
For love's the bridge, compassion's key,
To break the chains and finally be free.

5| The Insanity of a blank page

Inked Partners- Pen & Word once befriended me,
with hopes and promises of a bright future
warranting an outlet for life's odyssey.

One fine day,
The outlet was all choked up,
The erstwhile friends remained elusive,
A spectre in the shadows.

Years later, we have crossed paths again
Will this time be any different?

6| The Poetic Lens

Almost worried about making it sound like a cliché, I believe, both poetry and photography tend to be a common metaphor - life. Both these art forms tend to create something beautiful even if they represent a grotesque aspect of life.

That is to say, poetry or photography in itself, as an outcome, seems to carry a sense of allure, irrespective of the flavors of life it aims to give us a taste of. Many occasions have also brought to mind the thought that poetry and photography are imbibed in each other and aren't two separate art forms, which is to say that photography is a wordless poetry, eloquent nevertheless.

Being well-versed in basic medical terminologies, given the times we are living in, an analogy like this would make sense. Imagine photography as a booster dose of poetry. Surpassing the mind, its immediate impression is on the heart. This, of course, does not mean that one is better than the other.

Poetry bears comparison with photography in a sense that both are equally impactful and reflect an intricate metaphor called life in all facets.

7| The Real Evolution

How many lifetimes does it take for a person to realize, 'all that they frantically run behind is just as temporary as they are?'

Heck! You don't even get to take which you are most possessive about. The body that you once inhabited is either burnt or buried. We exhaust our lives aiming for all that ultimately comes with a time cap. In all this, we pay no heed to the accessory that lies within our bodies. The only commodity that can transgress even death - our soul.

Contemplating about the soul has also brought forth the idea that maybe it isn't the humans who evolve. Because if they did, the feelings of hatred, animosity, and a bunch of other "primitive" feelings would've become history. No, humans are just containers of souls. Instead of rampantly running behind things that are as temporary as us, why not strive to work on nourishing and bettering our souls instead?

After all, it is the only thing we get to take with us after death and possibly into a new body.

The previous pages were under construction for
2 years.
The contractor (aka, the author's brain) was on
an extended coffee break.

8| The Apparent Contrast

What if;
The play of thesis and antithesis,
The polarity of objects,
The seeming contradiction between situations,
Is it nothing but an illusion?
Or maybe our inability to look at the bigger picture?

It's like the waves of the ocean,
The tide and the ebb together create the waves.
Or like sunrise and sunset,
The combination of which completes a day.

Perhaps, like childhood and parenthood,
The phases that can never be exclusive of one
another.

How about,
The opposite genders,
The yin and yang, known to balance each other?

Or like hope and despair,
The two being equally essential to the experience of
being a human.

Maybe like past and the present,
The culmination of two foreshadows the future to come.

Maybe the idea of opposites is just a delusion.
And, after all,
It is like the two ends of the same spectrum.

9| Open letter to Rajkot

Dear Rajkot,

Addressing a letter to you feels weird. No, not because you're a city. You're much more than that. I would say, you're an emotion but I guess that would be too dramatic. All those who have spent the majority of their growing up years in your lap wouldn't help but to agree, when I say that you've come to resemble a safe haven for us over the years. We seldom value things, people, and places when we have them. Only their absence makes us realize that they have become an indispensable part of our lives. That is why writing a letter to you feels weird because we took you for granted and never anticipated that one day, we would miss you the most.

Dear Rajkot, while we were in your cocoon, we complained of your insufficiency. Strangely enough, we now crave the same insufficiency which made our lives simple. It's only when we have moved away from you, into the chaotic lives of the larger cities, did we realize what a laid-back town you are. After all, no other city has the custom of complete closure merely for sleeping! Who knew that over the years, the circumference of the Race Course would mean different things to different people? From playing the role of a mini-amusement park for kids to providing a place of "hangout" for teens and working as a reunion spot for adults, it has been a "go-to" place for all of us. Unlike the other cities that have ascended great levels of progress in terms of infrastructure and technology, you are still treading your way to the top, slowly.

Even though your pace of development may have been a cause of concern at some point, we have come to realize that, by far, you are the safest city in our state which is more than anything we could ever ask of you. The feeling of not belonging is a rarity in your case because the city as a whole is more like a closely-knit family. In larger cities, it is possible to blend into the crowd and go unnoticed but in your case, it is almost next to impossible. Wherever you go, whether you like it or not, you are bound to come across someone you know!

GALAXY
MOVIE
POSTERS

By now, you must have realized that the whole point of writing a letter to you has been about reminiscing the good old days and thanking you for providing us with all that you have.

Thank you for being a city that we can fondly call HOME.

10| Handle with care

Words.

One need not personify them, because that would mean abstractly assigning them qualities of the living while they're actually not. No, words are as alive as the next person you come across while reading this. A number of rhetorics should suffice to explain how.

Do words not have the power to be remembered years later, when the only thing retained in your memory would be what they spoke and not what they wore or how they looked?

Do words not possess the capacity to lead or mislead the person, depending on their use?

Aren't words sufficient enough to provoke or pacify people, again depending upon the context?

Is it not the fine usage of vocabulary that leads us to be mesmerized by someone or something?

Isn't it true that not all things are better left unsaid? The answers to these are insignificant, but what they stand to signify is something to think about. Words have the power to exercise independent control over an individual's thoughts and emotions just like any dominant person would have over the others, which makes them existential. It's all a matter of power struggle.

Do you control words or do words control you?

Our life provides an answer to this.

11| 69th Republic Day

India is a cradle of the human race,
The birthplace of human speech,
The mother of history,
The grandmother of legend, and the great
grandmother of tradition.
Mark Twain

68 years ago, on this day, the cradle of the human race was declared a Republic. The long-cherished reins of power were now handed over to us – the people of India. The most clichéd definition of a REPUBLIC that we often come across is a state in which people's will and wish reign supreme. This REPUBLIC Day instead of applauding ourselves for our achievements of the past 68 years, let us introspect to what extent we have lived up to that definition. How far have we the people, who claim to be our own masters, actually succeeded in freeing ourselves of any kind of bondage or compulsion? To what extent have we done justice to the idea of a Republican nation?

George Orwell once said, "If liberty means anything at all, it means the right to tell people what they do not want to hear." I think this statement holds a greater relevance in today's time where the slightest remark causes our volatile sentiments to take over our reasoning and leads us to act impulsively. One piece of historical fiction, one statement in support of our next-door neighbour or one post on the social media has the power to flush all our moral values down the drain and become a part of a mob - a mob hurtling abuses at the offender, a mob disrupting the working of a state or a mob threatening to kill.

But not all hope is lost.

On the flip side are those who live by the words of George Orwell. Those who have the courage to voice the truth in spite of threats. Those who remember that diversity is what defines India. Those who remember that freedom of speech, thought and expression is the core of who we are as a nation. In an age where the intolerant minority has so many venues to spread dissent, it is doubly necessary for the tolerant majority to speak up.

The second most important aspect of a Republican nation such as India is Justice. Sometimes, all that a rebellious child needs is love and attention. The insurgents in the north-eastern states are those rebellious children of India who have either been continually ignored or suppressed. They battle each day for the mere acknowledgment of their presence as well as to become a part of the national mainstream. Regular violation of human rights, migration issues, widespread poverty and a variety of such problems are a part of their everyday grim reality.

On a daily basis they battle for equality, liberty, justice and fraternity– rights they have been promised under the Indian constitution. And it is here that we must introspect why we celebrate Republic Day every year. It is not because of the splendour of the national parade or speeches fuelled by patriotic fervour.

We celebrate it because it is on this day that we the people of India made the momentous decision of choosing democracy over the other forms of government, choosing a constitution which would form our core values that we would adhere to and abide by over the years.

A democracy is not just the freedom to express dissent or consensus or the right to choose your leaders. It is also the freedom to assert what you stand for. It is finding your voice within a collective whole.

A nation is a reflection of the people who live in it. But do we want a country where the freedom to disagree isn't valued? Or a system where the individual isn't respected as an individual? Our democracy is like a legacy and identity for us and for generations to come - a check against totalitarian thought and autocratic functioning. So, let us celebrate republic day by embracing the ideals of our constitution and continue to strive along the path of becoming a true republic.

12| Morality- The art of minding someone else's business

She woke up one day.

It all began with her falling off to sleep
After being heavily drugged with MORALITY.
And thus, she slept to herself and woke up to the world.
Here began her life of principles and subtexts.

Started believing that everyone should be treated fair
The subtext being – only those who do not pose a threat to her

Decided to help those in need
The subtext being – forcing her 'help' on especially those who do not ask for it

Practised considering things from everyone's perspectives
The subtext being – only accepting those that befit her

Greeted everyone with a smile
The subtext being – even a fake one would do

Carried out a daily ritual of complimenting everyone
in order to 'make their day'
The subtext being – whether she genuinely meant it
or not

Preached about how one must not interfere in
someone's life
The subtext being – prying under the mask of
concern

Vouched for reality being multidimensional
The subtext being – created one of her own if the
actual didn't make sense

Passionately stood against the idea of gossiping and rumours
The subtext being – though a 'healthy discussion' is a must

Insisted the importance of looking goodness in everyone
The subtext being – practised the same as per her convenience

She woke up one day,
And realized, she had been sleeping all the while.
Realized, she had done it all wrong.
Realized, goodness was something that came naturally
Unlike MORALITY that required her to 'practice' being good
Realized that the MORALITY she was so fond of
Was just another gate-pass into the lives of anyone but herself.

"Managed goodness is not goodness at all.
It is pseudo, it is pretension, it is hypocrisy."

-A wise man

13| Hope's enduring flame

A fragile thread, hope, spun from dreams unseen,
A beacon in the stormy night,
A verdant isle in the oceans vast and keen,
A phoenix rising from despair's dark plight.

It is the whisper in the howling gale,
The flicker in the dying ember's core,
A steadfast anchor when everything else will fail,
The open door when pathways seem to close and pour.

Hope is the alchemist, turning grief to gold,
Transforming shadows into morning's light,
A story yet untold, a tale to be told,
A promise of tomorrow, pure and bright.

14| The plea of rivers

You. Yes you! The Human Race.
You are a paradox.
You sing songs about my purity.
You claim that I came down from heaven.
You believe that one dip in my vast bed can free you from all your wrongdoings.
Yet, you are a victim of habits.
Time and again you have made me, the element of heaven, experience hell on earth.
Every day millions of 'YOU' exploit my purity by using me as a garbage dump or a natural washing machine
You have misused me, past the endurance of any living being.

Dear Humans, I am the birthplace of civilizations
It is 'I' who quench your thirst,
who subside your hunger
Who keeps you clean and hydrated.
All that I ask is some empathy
You don't need to do great things for me
You could grow trees near my banks or simply not throw things in me.
And believe me, in the end, it is 'YOU' who is going to be the biggest beneficiary.

Dear Humans, it is 'YOU' who devised the saying
'Actions speak louder than words.'
It's about time you realize, your songs of my beauty and purity will mean nothing as long as your actions continue to suggest otherwise.

15| If found, please return

'What is the most precious thing you've lost over the years?' a man once asked.
I replied.

I was a child once
Until growing up became mandatory

Innocence was my area of dominance
Until the army of shrewdness invaded

Stupidity came naturally to me
Until intelligence was artificially injected
Creativity was like a pair of shoes that went along with every dress
Until the dress called examination refused
to go with it

Emptying the bottle of emotions by crying
was a habit
Until a lid to subdue the outflow was provided

Screaming to the lung's fullest capacity upon hearing a horror story was instinct
Until pretending to be bold for reputation became essential

Stubbornness to get 'that pink balloon' was the only known way
Until someone introduced the concept of compromising

Talking my heart out to express joy over trifles was always welcomed
Until the art of appreciation was lost into oblivion

Laughing out loud over the lamest of jokes signified carefree attitude
Until 'simply smiling' became a sign of sophistication

Thanking God before every meal was a lesson taught in every moral science class
Until eating like a robot to save time was encouraged in every Corporate Bible

Giving parents, bear hugs each night was the best
feeling in the world
Until being embarrassed just by their presence
kicked in

Sleeping for as long as the heart desired was a norm
Until sleeping only to avoid dark circles became
a requirement

Loving unconditionally was the only condition
heard of
Until 'Terms and Conditions' replaced the above.

What is the most precious thing that I've lost over
the years?
'The younger me.'

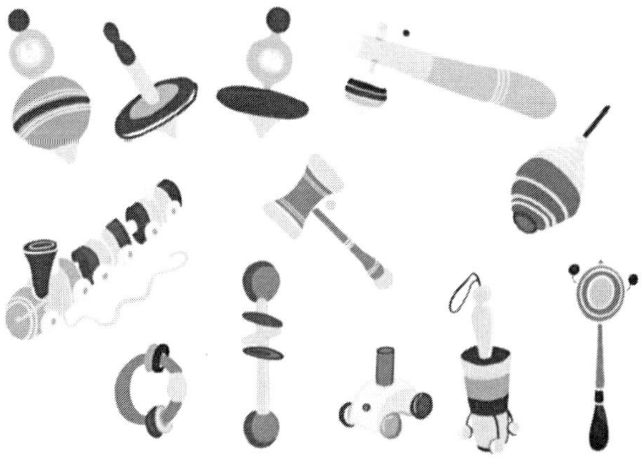

16| The Ha-ha funny world

The world is a funny place
You laugh too much, you shall be called mad
You laugh too little, you shall be called sad
The world is a funny place
You'll be tagged secretive if your tongue is short
Or talkative is your brand, if you're talking a lot
The world is a funny place
If you work too hard, you are deemed ambitious
If you work too little, you are condemned aimless
The world is a funny place
You speak up, arrogant is the word
You hold your tongue, you're a coward
The world is a funny place
Worrywart you'll be termed, if you worry too much
Careless will be your pet
name, if you don't worry as such
The world is a funny place
A gossip you are, if you talk about others
Selfish you are, if you talk about your brothers
A funny place is the World
You cry over trifles, you become over-sentimental
Stifle a cry and you shall be called cold-hearted
The world is a funny place
Impatient you'll be nicknamed, if you can't sit still

But if you simply sit at one place, lazy is your bill
Why does the world judge?
Confused, so utterly confused, such grudge!
The World is a funny, funny place.

17| Dissonance of the Soul

They preach of a divine lineage, a cosmic kinship, proclaiming all as God's progeny. Yet, the echoes of doubt whisper, 'Do they truly encompass the ebony hues of humanity within this grand tapestry of creation?'

Knowledge, they assert, is the sceptre of power, a crown worn by the enlightened. But what of those relegated to the margins, denied the ink to script their destinies? Do they not yearn for the same intellectual dominion?

Unity, a fortress against adversity, they proclaim. But does this bulwark extend beyond the confines of shared belief? Or is it a sanctuary exclusive to the like-minded?

The sword of knowledge, a double-edged blade, they contend. Yet, those who dare to wield it with truth as its hilt often find themselves wounded by the treacherous hands of power.

Verbosity is a common currency, exchanged freely. But actions, tangible and profound, are the gold standards by which legacies are forged. It is in the chasm between these two that the true measure of humanity resides.

18| Human's first

Indeed, there is a caste system in the world - Male and Female. So, today is a big day for the latter. International Women's Day!

I congratulate all the women on, well, being a woman - a role that demands 'multi-tasking' to be an ingrained quality.

I would like to grab this opportunity to share something that I've been dying to share (not literally), ever since I attended my friend's book launch and heard one of the prominent lady figures talk about feminism.

The person who believes and fights for equal rights for women is entitled to be called a feminist. Some of the radical feminists today have developed a tendency to take the chivalrous term 'ladies first' a little too seriously.

God created two types of humans; the former being termed as HE and the latter, SHE. Ever wondered why he had to create two different types of humans and not just one? It could've saved him a whole lot of time, energy and resources if only he had created one type of human. In any case, both were expected to do the same mundane tasks on this planet. But no, the 'he-knows-it-all' had to differentiate. Why? Because both have to play different roles on this planet and no one actor can replace the other.

While the "HE" may have to act as a protector of the family by being courageous and fighting, wherever required, the "SHE" may have to act as the protector of the family by radiating love. And just in case, being loving and supportive and not being able to act like "HE" during times of crisis sounds like a menial job, let me tell you, acting as a support system is another form of courage.

"Real courage is not a man with a gun in his hand"

Harper Lee

(Yes, I'm madly in love with that book)

I do not disagree with the fact that, in spite of the maddening wave of modernization, women in some parts of the world are denied equal rights with men.

Yes, women do deserve to be treated equally. They deserve to be treated equally just as another human being would be and not simply because they are women.

Having said this, I have a terrific idea (you can of course decide whether it's terrific or not). Let's change the term "Feminists" to "Humanists" instead. Its definition could be - A person who believes and fights for the equal rights of HUMANS. And yes, while we are redefining feminism, why not redefine the term 'equality' too?

As stated in one of my previous articles, differences are what makes us unique. We need not fight for superiority or as a matter of fact, equality in everything men do. We the "SHE" have our own set of purposes on this planet, and hence, let's embrace and take pride in that fact.

Happy Women's Day!

(Can we also change it to International Human's Day?

Haha! I know I'm getting on your nerves.)

19| Because apparently, we live in a democracy

'Atticus Finch,' the first name that came to my mind the moment I read the news of Gurmehar Kaur and her statement that managed to set the country ablaze with criticism. 'To Kill a Mockingbird' by Harper Lee is one of the finest pieces of literary work in the world today. In the novel, Atticus Finch, a white lawyer is severely criticized when he chooses to defend an innocent black man and is termed as "nigger-lover."

Fast forward to 2017, India, where some of the 'tolerant,' 'unbiased,' 'open-minded,' and here's a better word, 'modern' Indians lashed out at her because, her statement had apparently made them feel insecure, and gave out the feel that she was in support of Pakistan. But then, what if she was in support of Pakistan? Don't we live in Democracy which grants the freedom of speech and expression to all its citizens. Oh yes, that reminds me, that those out there threatening her don't seem to realise that they are violating the fundamental right of an Indian citizen, which at least constitutionally stands punishable by law.

Now, let's look at it like this. Her exact words were 'Pakistan did not kill my dad, war killed him.' Does it anywhere mention, 'I am in support of Pakistan?'

It's all about the way you look at things. I choose to believe that she was not supporting Pakistan. Instead, she was opposing the idea of war. Now, some of us may also have a tendency to equate 'WAR' with 'PAKISTAN.'

Imagine your father works in an organization which comprises mainly immoral people. Your father, of course, isn't one of them. You overhear people severely criticizing the organization and blatantly accusing every single person working there to be immoral. Wouldn't you, the daughter/son of your innocent father, retaliate that one cannot generalize? How then can we generalize that Pakistan is a terrorist? It is also made up of people. People who love peace, those who cannot stand the idea of war.

Oh, and did you know that the war of 1999 was fought between India and Pakistan? Did you catch that? Oh, silly me! I bet you already knew that. Clapping requires the efforts of both the hands. The war was fought between India and Pakistan. So, it really wasn't only Pakistan that killed Gurmehar's father.

Whatever it may be, one thing is for sure. Yes, Gurmehar was against it. She was against the idea of proving one's superiority by causing death and destruction. It seems as if, sometimes, people are so used to thinking the 'Wrong', that they lose their sense of distinguishing the 'Right.' Criticism is always rewarded to the people who show the courage to challenge the ideas of a majority, irrespective of being right or wrong.

20| Excavated Truth- A short story

"Karam knows it all!" whispered Megha. Dhruvi was a newcomer and Megha was supplying her with a one-line introduction of each passerby which was usually something negative. But this was miraculous! For the first time, in the last half an hour, Megha uttered something positive about a passer-by.

This intrigued Dhruvi and she inquired, "What is so different about him?"

Megha began, "Karam is an epitome of a perfect employee. He has abundance of knowledge and wisdom and in spite of that, he is down to earth and a happy go lucky person. Most employees can't decide whether to be jealous of him or fascinated by him. And what's more, the boss loves him!"

He was probably the only person who had been bestowed with the honour of being praised by Megha, the critic, thought Dhruvi. A year passed by in a puff of dust, and the winds of destiny were in her favour. Her hard work and consistency had borne her the fruits of promotion twice.

Her mother would've been proud to see her daughter so successful. But little did she know that destiny does not oscillate only in one direction.

Just when Dhruvi's life seemed at the peak of perfection, her only reason for life on earth passed away. She was in the middle of a presentation when she was told that her father had passed away due to cardiac arrest. His death created a vacuum in her life. Her mother had passed away while bringing her into the world, and now, her father had passed away after getting her acquainted with the world. Slowly and steadily, she managed to tread the race of life.

People began noticing the deteriorating condition of Dhruvi. One day, the boss called her as well as Karam to his office. The meeting went on for an hour and all the employees kept glancing at his office door in anticipation. Anything involving the two of the best employees of the office always ignited a spark among them. To their delight, Dhruvi finally came out of the cabin, and instantly people swarmed around her. 'What happened?' asked one. 'Is it another promotion?' chimed in another.

Before Dhruvi could respond to any of their questions, the Boss and Karam walked out of the office which quietened everyone. Once again, Dhruvi retreated to her den and resumed her work.

Days passed by, and people started noticing a new trend. Everyday Karam would come to the office, talk to Dhruvi for a couple of minutes and then walk away minding his own business. The employees could've made it to the Guinness book for the number of hypotheses they came up with. Some said that Karam and Dhruvi were once again going to be promoted while others reasoned that maybe they were working on a secret project assigned by the boss who always favoured them. However, all of them were of one common opinion. Something fishy was happening for sure. They didn't know what but wanted to find it out by hook or crook.

Megha couldn't stand Dhruvi's rise to fame. "I just can't let that newcomer have all the glory in the world. She has already been promoted twice, and now, she is also working with Karam on something. I have to do something." The next day the atmosphere of the office had reached its boiling point.

As soon as Dhruvi stepped into the office, the predators were ready to poach her with their vicious rumours. Rumours had it that Dhruvi and Karam were seeing each other and the boss had called them to warn them of their misconduct. Karam and Dhruvi were shocked out of their minds when they discovered this. However, they couldn't retaliate against anyone as per the instructions of their boss.

This continued for weeks and the atmosphere of the office kept worsening. Whenever Karam or Dhruvi passed by an employee, one person would make a joke on them, while the others would contribute through their laughter. One day, when all this was happening the boss came out of his office, and the truth told by him shook up everyone's conscience.

The truth was that Dhruvi had been suffering from depression due to her father's death. She had no family, and all her relatives were abroad. The boss considered Dhruvi his daughter and asked Karam to be friends with her, and accompany her to a psychiatrist to fight depression. It was with Karam's help that Dhruvi was finally making progress. "Each one of you are actually cowards.

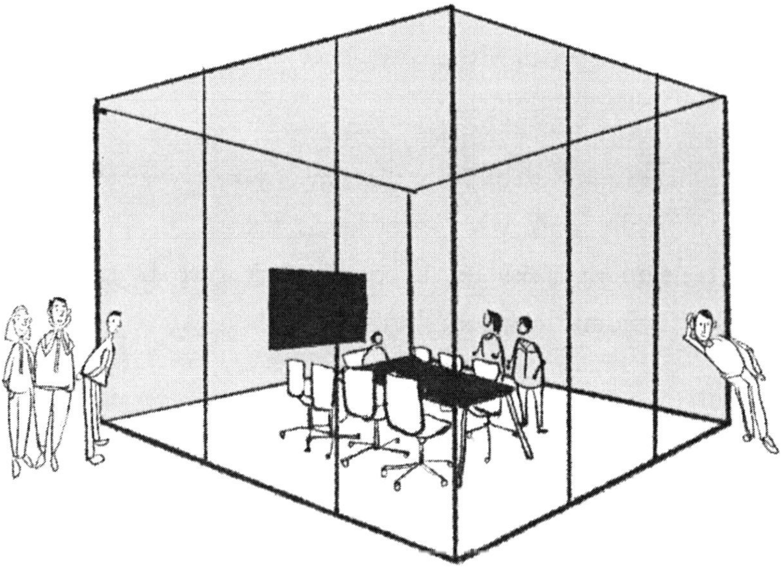

As soon as you saw a fresh piece of gossip, very conveniently you forgot Dhruvi's tragedy. I feel ashamed to call you all my employees," said the boss.

Megha still did not have the guts to accept that she was the biggest culprit of all. It was she who had started the worst rumour out of jealousy. Nevertheless, she too was a human with a conscience and her guilt made her resign from the job.

Dhruvi and Karam, from that day onwards, were able to finally walk with their heads held high. Their continuous visits to the psychiatrist gave Dhruvi finally someone whom she could call family.

21| Himalayan Harmony

Throned in emerald depths where silence weaves,
A symphony of nature softly seeps.
Beside me, busy bees' chorus hum,
While cawing crows in raucous accents come.
Tiny birds, a sweet and subtle choir,
Join, in the woodland's melody entire.

Beyond this green, where forest shadows creep,
Stand mountains, crowned in winter's icy sleep.
Their grandeur etched in hues of purest white,
Defies all words, a breath-taking sight.
Unyielding giants, steadfast, strong and still,
Beneath the weight of heaven's frozen spill.

22| Ephemeral Moments

How swiftly time's river sweeps away,
An ancient query, none can fully say.
Not merely minutes, hours, months that part,
But what they symbolize within the heart.

"Life goes on," the wise ones gravely state,
A river flowing through each shifting fate.
Yet, does it chart the same course through each land?
It moves, but change touches every strand.

For as Heraclitus softly hints in rhyme,
One cannot step in the same river twice.
So, life continues, with its subtle chime,
Ever flowing, changing, yet precise.

23| The curious case of the other

We often find ourselves strangely drawn to the lives of others. A glimpse into someone else's world is a forbidden fruit that tempts our curiosity. Yet, the moment we reach for it, cries of invasion echo. It's a peculiar paradox - we crave secrets but condemn those who seek them.

Gossip, the currency of social interaction, flows freely. We relish the lives of others, dissecting their choices with ruthless glee. But beneath this facade of disinterest, a deeper question lingers - why? If we truly care so little, why spend energy on their affairs? Is it perhaps a mask for our insecurities, a way to feel superior by magnifying another's flaws? Or could it be that in the shadows of their lives, we find a convenient escape from examining our own?

24| Looking good at any cost- A short story

"Daddy, when I've grown up, I want to be the best-looking model in the world!" exclaimed Natasha. This statement from a nine-year-old ought to make most parents happy. However, the opposite was true in Natasha's case. Natasha was a lonely child. Her only companions were her adoring parents and a busy television set. Society seldom accepted her.

How did this happen? Natasha was a victim of a terrible skin disease that would stick with her for the rest of her life. Her parents confronted her monstrous fate with great strength. For them, she was and would always remain their "little bundle of joy".

As time progressed, and Natasha grew up, she started sensing that the "OTHERS" refrained from conversing with her. "THEY" considered her poles apart from what they were. Nevertheless, it mattered to her. The question of whether it should have or not still remains a mystery. If we would've been there, we would've said, "Hey, how does it even matter? People just talk." Yes, people just talk. But had we been in her shoes, we would've realized how being an outcast felt like. Every single day she battled with one question. Why was she so different and what was her mistake in that?

One day, as she was about to enter her class, the daily ritual of mockery enraged her to an extent that for the very first time, she decided to get back to them. With seething eyes she shouted, "One day, I will be the prettiest model in the world!" Indeed, her childhood desire had never left her.

Natasha's dream ballooned during the sophomore years. She envied all the "gorgeous" girls of the college who received all the attention. On the next most fateful day of her life, she came across an advertisement which she thought could make her dream true. Dr. Newman Washington, the world-famous doctor, could cure any skin disease for 2 crore rupees, said the advertisement. The advertisement carried pictures of top models who had successfully undergone the pathbreaking treatment.

Ecstatically, Natasha rushed to her parents and begged them to show her case to Dr. Newman. Her parents were reluctant at first. They tried timidly explaining to her that it was a hoax. But Natasha wouldn't budge. All she stubbornly repeated was, "I want to look good at any cost." As she was their only child, they gave in to her demand finally.

Most people confess that one should never lose hope. However, the parents had lost all hope after their beloved child committed suicide soon after her unsuccessful surgery. To some of their inquisitive relatives who tried to find tender reasons for Natasha's suicide, her parents softly answered, "She had a desire which even God wouldn't fulfil." "What?" they asked. Together the sad parents replied, "To look good at any cost."

This simple story portrays the saddest truth of the life faced by people who constantly feel that they don't look "good enough."

25| The Oh-so weird norms!

A couple of days ago, my pal came back from her trip to Italy. One of the experiences shared by her caught my eye. According to her, the people there did not have any 'maids.' They themselves managed their household chores or hired a 'professional' which as per our Indian norm is a 'maid.' In this case, not only are the names different, the way in which they are treated is also different.

We Indians just cannot do without 'maids.' The 'not-so-clean' people whom we usually look down upon ironically are the ones who tidy up our places every morning.

This is bizarre! I call it our "Oh-so-weird-norm" Let us analyse one more example. It's about those who despise the non-vegetarians.

I remember my primary school textbook had a line:

"All plants around us are LIVING CREATURES.
They cannot move yet they are alive."

The above sentence explicitly tells us that plants as well as animals are living. So, why hate the non-vegetarians when you yourself are doing the same? I'm certain that you too must've come across one or the other "Oh-so weird-norms".

26| Where the mind is without fear

"Like animals in a zoo
I'll be slave to principles not men
The clergy and false, I condemn
My thoughts shall not be ruled
My rights shall not be fooled"

- Yash Ramchandani

Most of us today aren't aware of the fact that we are deprived of the privilege to think. Yes, you read it right! We are deprived of the privilege to think. Why? Because right from the time we step into this world our thoughts are influenced or rather conditioned by the society we reside in. For instance, remember the time when you were told not to "cry like a girl?" This was the time when the notion of "girls are supposedly weaker than boys" was drilled into your vulnerable brains. This was the time when we did not have the ability to question the norms of the society and so we accepted the "idea" without giving it a second thought.

However, this is just an example. Even as adults there are times when our thoughts contradict those of our fellow mates. But guess what? We feel that we are doing a moronic thing and readily join the thought process of people around us. Up to a certain age, our mind absorbs whatever is instilled in it without differentiating good from bad. Nevertheless, as we grow up our mind starts questioning things. Sadly, the so-called "experienced" people around us ask us to snap out of it.

The actual problem with us is that we are always convinced that what "they" say ought to be right. Our mind is like a bird in a cage which longs for freedom. Freedom of mind is the greatest gift one can give to himself/herself. The day this gift is received, it would bring victory with trumpets of triumph blowing to the thought of our Indian Nobel laureate Rabindranath Tagore's, "Where the mind is without fear, the head is held high."

27| Chitranagri- The jewel in the crown of our city

What is the first thing that comes to your mind when I say 'public places' or specifically 'public walls?' Old worn-out paint, weird things scribbled on the walls, paan ki pichkari and so on... Right?

Well, it's time to reconsider your opinions because the walls in my city i.e. Rajkot has got a complete makeover. Yes, a mesmerising makeover! Some time back the 'Smart City Trust' of Rajkot launched a project called 'Chitranagri' and since then the people of my city have taken up the task of beautifying the walls across the city by painting their imagination.

Colors are something that fascinate a child and an adult alike. By painting the walls across the town our city has been bestowed with numerous benefits like a control over the people spoiling walls, appreciation and a visit by the team of 'Taarak Mehta', eye-catching walls and hopefully by the end of this project a name in the Guinness Book of world records!

Now every Sunday, instead of waking up at noon, saying “Aaje to Ravivar che (Today is Sunday)”, and gobbling up dhokla, fafda and jalebi, the people of Rajkot enthusiastically participate in the wall painting programs at various locations. Of course, all this is impossible without a strong backbone. The “Chitranagri team” works tremendously hard to provide this backbone.

They inform people, register names, provide the painting kit, stay on toes at the site in order to supervise as well as provide extra colors, collect the painting kit back, write and distribute certificates. Humph! Seems like a lot of work doesn’t it? But this is just a summary, they do much more than this.

Another thing that I’ve been able to conclude after participating in this project is that it has converted our town into one big family. Wherever you go for painting the walls you’ll experience people offering refreshments as well as any help required and also showering the participants with tons of appreciation.

As it is rightly said that "You have your brush, you have your colors, you paint paradise." We Rajkotians have created our own unique paradise. All thanks to Mr.Jitubhai Gotecha, Shri Vijay Nehra, Mr. Maulikbhai Gotecha and all those who have contributed generously towards this project. Afterall, our city isn't called Rangilu Rajkot for no reason.

28| The road less travelled

"Khete hai agar kisi cheez ko dil se chaho ...To puri kainaat use tumse milane ki koshish mei lag jaati hai"

So, how many SRK fans here? Every once in a while, we all go wild for that one 'jalak' of our favourite celebrities, don't we? But what when someone tells us that they've taken up 'Humanities.' We act as if they've started inhaling carbon dioxide instead of oxygen! This is ironic, isn't it? "Acting" itself is a part of the Humanities stream!

Ever since I've taken up humanities, I've come across a lot of amusing comments like, "Ohmigod! Why Humanities ya? You were so intelligent?" or something like, "Group A or Group B?" and when I break the news that I've taken up arts they are shocked out of their minds. Seriously, the facial expressions are worth watching.

For all those who criticize humanities, I request you to take a break and think for yourself... What would life be without entertainment? Won't the cricket matches be boring without a commentator?

And the best of all is... You would be living in the 19th century if it weren't for news reporters!

Do we ever wish to get a 'jalak' from any doctor? Heck, we don't even have any such thing as a favourite doctor. Moreover, the very mention of a doctor makes most of us flee. How many of us admire Mr. Amitabh Bachchan, Harsha Bhogle, MF Hussain etc.

There won't be a person in India who isn't familiar with these names. But how many of you are familiar with the five best C. As for your town. Hardly any. See there lies the difference. Not everyone is good with physics or biology but at the same time not everyone requires these subjects to achieve greatness in life. This does not mean that I've got any grudges against the commerce or science students. All I want is people to realise that "Humanities" is not associated with "losers," instead it is for those who have the courage to choose the path less travelled.

"Science is what the society aspires,
Humanities is what my heart desires"
-The Humanities Students

29| Eureka! I just discovered what comes after eternity

Arghh! I think I just found out what comes after "eternity." Put on your seatbelts people... What follows eternity is "nothingness." Yeah, I know I sound totally dumb. See that's the reason I asked you to put on your seatbelts so that you don't fall down while laughing hard at my insanity. But no, I'm not talking gibberish. When the board exams first started, I felt that it would be something like "Ta-da! It was just yesterday and so soon it's over."

Sadly, my predictions suffered a terrible fate. Just when I felt that exams had been going on for eternity I realized that "eternity" too had its limits. What followed it was a state in which you don't feel like studying or rather revising even if you have exams the next day. I termed it as "nothingness."

One day prior to my first paper, people were flooding into my home and showering me with best wishes and most importantly CHOCOLATES.

At that time, I thought "Hey, if that's the sort of priority you get just

for appearing on the "boards" I wouldn't mind appearing every year." Ha-ha! Of course I had to be wrong. It's actually the sort of priority you get when people know that you are about to get caught up in the hurricane of madness. No offence to my well-wishers though.

Duh it's going to be SEVEN more days for the examiners to be finally done with us.

P.S. The best part? No more maths after that (Possibly forever)

30| A new expedition

Few years back, it was predicted by some people that the world would meet a disastrous end by 2012, but guess what? It's been years now and we're still ALIVE! Today's "Times Life" had some very amazing lines that were an eye opener for me and that's what inspired me to write this....

"Rightly understood, the New Year festival is an act of faith. It is easier for the year to change than to change ourselves. But we believe that somehow, magically, one will lead to the other."

These beautiful lines by R.Joseph Hoffmaan contain such a great meaning. Every new year the magazines, newspapers, websites etc are filled with tons of ideas on making our new year fantabulous. But how long are we able to follow them? New Year resolutions hardly survive a month at the most. I think new years are simply created by humans to assure themselves that they have plenty of opportunities to get what they desire for.

Like, "I may not succeed this year but next year I'm sure to breeze through this situation." At the same time, there are a few for whom each New Year calls for a new expedition. They constantly try to quench their thirst to learn something new, something different every year. So, this so-called new year, let us all try to get ourselves included in the category of those who actually make their stay on this planet worthy!

31| Differences make us unique

According to the Christian mythology, we are all the descendants of Adam and Eve. We all share a common creator, the colour of everyone's blood is red and of course we all are humans. What is it that makes us stand apart from the rest? I think it is our character, ideology and our talents that make us what we call unique. Just imagine a world wherein everyone is equal and works like a machine day in and day out. Now that sounds like our idea of a monotonous life, doesn't it?

I'm sure most of you must have heard the Amazon music, 'Aur dikhao, aur dikhao.' This shows that we all demand variety and that is exactly what we get in our real life. Some of us here may not be good at Mathematics (For instance: Myself) while others may be a champ at it. I think everyone is equally valuable because a shoemaker may not be literate but imagine what would happen if there were no shoemakers! I'm sure that the people who are obsessed with purchasing shoes every weekend would go haywire.

Similarly, we require comedians as much as we require doctors because when all the medicines fail to work, laughter is the only medicine that cures us. Now tell me, do we need any other reason to celebrate our differences?

32| Time's Up: Stop the blame game now!

Let me tell you a recipe. 1 tbsp. of poverty, a glass of dissatisfaction, a pinch of greed, a spoonful of desire for shortcuts and a gravy of various other negative aspects of society. I'm sure you must have guessed it by now. It's the recipe for the dish of corruption.

The other day, I came across an educated person who simply in order to take a shortcut and get a B.Ed. degree gave Rs.10,000 extra to the university and guess what? He was exempted from being regularly present to the university and was also assured a good percentage in exams. Normally, we get to hear about different incidents related to corruption but it's the first time I had someone right in front of my eyes who had done such a thing and was easily accepting it without any sense of guilt.

That's the reason why I felt like writing about corruption. We often blame "them" and claim ourselves to be innocent when asked what the real cause of corruption is. Here, "them" refers to politicians, government officials or any other person in the entire universe EXCEPT us! So, it's time to stop the blame game now. Accusing each other, fighting or merely preaching won't lead us anywhere. According to some cynical people, the evil of corruption is extremely powerful and cannot be eradicated easily.

Nevertheless, we are the youth of this nation. We can eradicate this evil through our optimism, honesty, dedication, hard work and want of justice. If Indians can successfully carry out the exploration on Mars, then removing the roots of corruption is going to be a piece of cake. We need to put on our armour and get into the battlefield with this demon. As it is rightly said, "Action speaks louder than words." The foremost way in which corruption can be demolished is by restricting our own self from indulging in any such kind of dirty tricks. Moreover, when we come across any such situation, we need to act.

For my part, I made sure to let that person know that they had made a very big blunder. Furthermore, I also played my part by sharing this with you people and spreading awareness.

#FightAgainstCorruption

33| Feeling Ecstatic

A teacher, as the oxford dictionary describes is someone who teaches in school. Well, is this all it has to say? I was quite shocked when I discovered this. How can the meaning of such a precious word be presented so bluntly? Ask a student the meaning and value of their Guru and I'm sure they'll be able to write a thesis for the same.

Today, on the occasion of teacher's day, I feel blessed to have one of the best teachers in the entire world, Jasmine Ma'am. English has always been my favourite subject and maybe it's because I've always had good teachers for the same but no one can be compared to Jasmine Ma'am. She's a cut above the rest. This may sound like an exaggeration to some of you but I'm sure every student, once during their life, shall or would have experienced the influence of a good teacher. My teacher is my constant source of support and inspiration.

According to me, she is a paradigm of an amazing teacher. Usually, when people want to express how great someone is, they come up with "I don't have words to express...." How is it that we run short of vocabulary when we want to express how great someone is? In my case, I have a long list of words to describe my dear teacher. It goes on like this: Hardworking, Understanding, supportive, friendly, firm, smart, unique etc. The list is unending! Hey people, did you just notice that the above qualities are the ingredients that cook up a perfectionist?

That's exactly what my teacher is. She has the ability to keep the class captivated with her extraordinary real-life incidents. My teacher is special to me because she became my lighthouse and showed me the right path at some point of time. I'm thankful to my dear teacher for the same.

It made a huge difference in my life.

In today's era, you hardly find teachers who are extremely supportive, who constantly encourage you to do better and who apart from being a good teacher is also a good friend. I'm lucky to have one such teacher. Thank you for everything, ma'am. You are my guardian angel. Thanks, a billion.

34| Balloons on my mind

Balloons remind me of those long-lost childhood days! Suddenly, one day, they just vanished in a puff of dust, leaving behind those joyful memories of cartoons, toys, gifts etc. The list is unending!

A child with abundance of innocence is always eager to grow up but little does he realize what awaits him once he grows up. Of course, growing up is a wonderful experience in itself but nothing can compare those beautiful days. Somehow as we grow up, we suddenly stop living our life for ourselves, rather we get obsessed with what people think about us. We blindly start following the crowd without considering if it is right for us or not. As children, we live in a carefree manner. We do not bother about laughing insanely or crying over every small thing, but the moment we start growing up, we become a believer of etiquettes, rules etc. We become so self-conscious that at some instances, we feel ashamed of expressing our love and gratitude towards others. As it is rightly said, "It is mandatory to grow old but it is not compulsory to grow up."

It depends on us as to how we choose to live. Whether we choose to keep the child inside us always alive or we choose to grow up and completely forget, that once upon a time, we too were children.

35| Paper or Power

Benjamin Franklin once said, "Money has never made man happy, nor will it, there is nothing in its nature to produce happiness. The more of it one has the more one wants."

Money is a miracle of hard work, but at times, it is a curse of cheating. Usually, money can make a person go mad with happiness. In today's world, people crave money in order to meet their luxurious demands. Nowadays, people use it as a tool to flaunt their wealth but I believe that the real wealth lies in humanity. There are people who are even ready to work against humanity in order to earn. For a poor person 'money' is a 'luxury' that he hardly gets, for a middle-class man 'money' is his 'livelihood' and for a high-class man 'money' is a symbol of 'status'.

Money is a mere piece of paper that plays a vital role in our life, but in reality, it fails to buy the essential things of life such as love, kindness, trust etc. Money is ambrosia for those who know its proper usage and importance and sweet poison for those who don't. I believe that no one, anywhere, escapes the power of money. How we feel about money is central to how we live our lives.

36| Education: The Key to freedom

'Education is the tonic to ease the pain of ignorance'

According to me, education is an ornament that beautifies our brain, soul and character. It is something without which life is futile. It does not only include the knowledge of textbooks rather it is a wider concept which includes the knowledge of the surrounding environment, knowledge of day-to-day life of different people and also includes the knowledge of different challenges of life and ways to face them.

I believe that a person who is well equipped with knowledge will find surviving in today's era a complete breeze! In today's world, knowledge is the only powerful weapon that will help a person fight his/her way out of any situation.

Access to education is the right of each and every citizen of the world. Unfortunately, there are millions of people around the world who are deprived of the pleasures of learning. Lack of literacy leads to various social evils such as terrorism, wars etc. and education is the only cure for all this.

I also believe that education is something that is free of age barriers i.e. the process of learning is eternal. As it is rightly said, ‘Education is the key to unlock the golden doors of freedom’. It is this freedom that helps us realize our true potential.

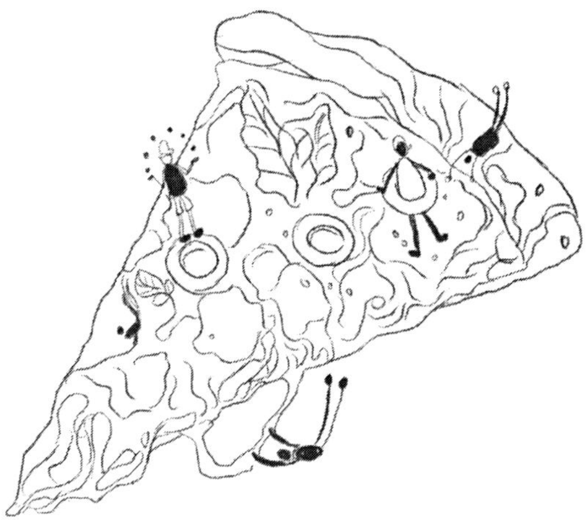

AFTERWORD

....

A decade is a generous slice of life. In this time, the world has transformed, reshaped itself with startling speed and complexity. Through these pages, a personal journey unfolds, one marked by growth, doubt, wonder, and a ceaseless pursuit of understanding. These words, once ephemeral digital imprints, now find a tangible form.

Each blog post, a snapshot frozen in time, reflects a specific moment, a particular emotion, a unique perspective. As I look back at these pieces, I am struck by the recurring themes, the evolving self, and the constant search for meaning. Yet, it is also the diversity of thoughts, the unexpected turns, and the raw vulnerability that give this collection its depth.

This book is not a definitive statement but an ongoing conversation. It is an invitation to connect, reflect, and find resonance in shared experiences. As life continues to unfold, so will the story. This collection is simply a chapter, a pause in the narrative, a moment to look back before turning the page.

ABOUT THE AUTHOR

....

As a versatile individual with a deep-rooted passion for arts, the author has cultivated a multifaceted career. Grounded in a Master's degree in English Literature, her lifelong affinity for storytelling has been a constant companion. Dubbed a 'bookworm' during her formative years, she has spent countless hours immersed in fictional worlds, a pursuit that ignited her creative spark.

Beyond the realm of literature, she has excelled in public communication, leveraging her natural charisma and eloquence. A period at a Barbadian radio station refined her ability to captivate audiences, a skill further honed through her experiences as an educator. These roles have allowed her to connect with diverse individuals, fostering a profound appreciation for the human experience.

Complementing her verbal artistry, the author possesses a keen eye for visual aesthetics. Drawing and photography serve as outlets for her creative expression, offering unique perspectives of the world around her. "Hues of Metanoia" is a testament to her ability to explore complex ideas through multiple artistic mediums, inviting readers into a world shaped by both intellect and imagination.